*Success Is for You: Using Heart-Centered Principles
for Lasting Abundance and Fulfillment*

*Transcending the Levels of Consciousness:
The Stairway to Enlightenment*

Truth vs. Falsehood: How to Tell the Difference

*The Wisdom of Dr. David R. Hawkins:
Classic Teachings on Spiritual Truth and Enlightenment*

Audio Programs

How to Surrender to God

Live Life as a Prayer

The Map of Consciousness Explained

Please visit:

Hay House UK: www.hayhouse.co.uk
Hay House USA: www.hayhouse.com®
Hay House Australia: www.hayhouse.com.au
Hay House India: www.hayhouse.co.in

In the World,
BUT NOT OF IT

Also by
David R. Hawkins, M.D., Ph.D.

Books

*Book of Slides: The Complete Collection Presented
at the 2002–2011 Lectures with Clarifications*

*Daily Reflections from Dr. David R. Hawkins:
365 Contemplations on Surrender, Healing,
and Consciousness*

*Discovery of the Presence of God:
Devotional Nonduality*

*The Ego Is Not the Real You: Wisdom to
Transcend the Mind and Realize the Self*

The Eye of the I: From Which Nothing Is Hidden

Healing and Recovery

I: Reality and Subjectivity

Letting Go: The Pathway of Surrender

*The Map of Consciousness Explained:
A Proven Energy Scale to Actualize Your Ultimate Potential*

*Power vs. Force: The Hidden
Determinants of Human Behavior*

Reality, Spirituality and Modern Man

In the World,

BUT NOT OF IT

Transforming
Everyday Experience into
a Spiritual Path

Dr David R. Hawkins

HAY HOUSE

Carlsbad, California • New York City
London • Sydney • New Delhi

Published in the United Kingdom by:
Hay House UK Ltd, The Sixth Floor, Watson House,
54 Baker Street, London W1U 7BU
Tel: +44 (0)20 3927 7290; Fax: +44 (0)20 3927 7291; www.hayhouse.co.uk

Published in the United States of America by:
Hay House Inc., PO Box 5100, Carlsbad, CA 92018-5100
Tel: (1) 760 431 7695 or (800) 654 5126
Fax: (1) 760 431 6948 or (800) 650 5115; www.hayhouse.com

Published in Australia by:
Hay House Australia Ltd, 18/36 Ralph St, Alexandria NSW 2015
Tel: (61) 2 9669 4299; Fax: (61) 2 9669 4144; www.hayhouse.com.au

Published in India by:
Hay House Publishers India, Muskaan Complex, Plot No.3, B-2,
Vasant Kunj, New Delhi 110 070
Tel: (91) 11 4176 1620; Fax: (91) 11 4176 1630; www.hayhouse.co.in

Cover design: Barbara LeVan Fisher
Interior design: Julie Davison

The moral rights of the author have been asserted.

A catalogue record for this book is available from the British Library.

Tradepaper ISBN: 978-1-78817-686-6
E-book ISBN: 978-1-4019-6506-8

Printed and bound in Great Britain by Clays Ltd, Elcograf S.p.A.

CONTENTS

INTRODUCTION

What does it mean to be "in the world, but not of it"? As spiritual aspirants we have probably heard of this saying and have asked, *How does this apply to me in my life, and is it really possible, especially in today's technological world, which can be hectic, confusing, and stressful at times?* As we attempt to evolve to higher awareness and consciousness, we may try applying a spiritual practice or a meditation or inspirational concepts in our daily lives, but how do we fulfill the demands of a spiritual life yet still keep up with the responsibilities of everyday living?

In this book, adapted from an audio presentation, Dr. David R. Hawkins helps us discover just that, and what this means for each one of us. By sharing his own experiences, giving his wise counsel, and talking honestly yet compassionately, he shows us that with intention and integrity, and a sense of humor, we *can* walk a spiritual path and, at the same time, live in the world without getting lost in it.

Living life in today's world is challenging, with so many distractions and additional pressures placed on us both internally and externally. Dr. Hawkins often stated that we can use the world to be free of the world and that life on Earth gives us the perfect opportunities for our greatest growth. You will learn more about this as you read through these chapters.

When the weight of the world feels heavy or overwhelming, Dr. Hawkins suggests that we "wear the world like a light garment."

As you read through this book, we hope that your fears will lessen and love will be more present, enlightening your path.

With blessings for your highest good,

Veritas Publishing

CHAPTER 1

Choosing the Spiritual Pathway

While modern technologies have provided a vast array of new toys and conveniences, the basic problems of human existence remain. In many ways, they've actually gotten worse. The hustle and bustle of daily life is accelerating at a breakneck speed. The human dilemma, in fact, is more confused than ever, and the very foundations of Western civilization have weakened under the onslaughts of rival factions and the constant media barrage. We've become like a giant focus group, continually being manipulated by the media.

But there is good news for people like you who have a desire to learn and grow spiritually. You are among a unique group that has the tools to not only survive, but to enjoy life and partake in all the beauty around you. You are in this world but not part of it.

The book you hold in your hands, from renowned spiritual teacher Dr. David Hawkins, explains why humankind has been lost in a house of mirrors and how we can escape it. Dr. Hawkins offers practices and tools to integrate this information into your everyday life.

Throughout, you'll experience the wisdom and humor of one of the world's greatest spiritual teachers.

— —

Jesus said to wear the world like a light garment. In other words, you notice it, you experience it, but it is not your ultimate destination—it's only transitory. The idea is to not sacrifice the soul for the mortal body. There is far more than this earthly life.

In today's world, we see how spiritual teachers have a higher level of consciousness. The head of the Catholic Church, Pope John Paul [II], calibrated on the Map of Consciousness™ at about 565, a level associated with joy and peace. Similarly, the Dalai Lama calibrates around 570. They've achieved that level due to a lot of internal, spiritual, and religious training. They radiate goodwill toward others.

The Challenges of the Spiritual Pathway

The difficulty is we're all dealing with a shared level of consciousness as well as our own individual levels. The collective level of consciousness goes up and down. Meanwhile, the problems remain the same. We continue to have the same obstacles to enlightenment, only modern man is at a greater disadvantage than before because of external forces. Programming by falsity is near constant. Just look at the way a commercial is put together: the rate of speed of the change of the images, and the subliminal programming. They show you the car and then they immediately show you an attractive person. They try to combine desire with lust and collapse several instinctual drives into one. The advertising for many products is weak. If you calibrate it, you'll see that not only does it not attract the view, it actually causes aversion.

Raising Your Consciousness Level

Interestingly, your happiness is not directly related to the external world at all. It's related to your inner level of consciousness. We see this in people who win the lottery and become multimillionaires overnight. Often, when people experience sudden fame and fortune and are unprepared for it, it destroys their happiness.

The correlation between happiness and level of consciousness is almost 100 percent. At certain levels of consciousness, it doesn't matter where you are, you're going to be happy and gratified, no matter what's going on. Your happiness is not dependent on external forces.

You've stopped placing importance on the external, the fame, the glamor.

For instance, a lot of young men want to grow up and become athletes, and they look at the most famous sports stars with such envy. They project that feeling onto the athlete.

When I grew up, being an athlete was the *last* thing I wanted. I wanted to get straight A's and finish a book a day. I read at least 500 books a year and I made copious notes on each book. My interests were of a different nature altogether in which physicality played little or no part.

Fortunately, my desire to learn and understand the world was fulfilled by my intellectual capabilities. If you become aware of the consciousness of the Buddha, then nothing less than that will satisfy you. You find yourself on a spiritual journey—a calling—to read all the great spiritual treatises and absorb their wisdom.

At a very young age, I experienced enlightened states of consciousness and a profound understanding of the nature of divinity as the presence of infinite love beyond all time, beyond all limitation. As a teenager, I experienced the Self with a capital S in a completely nonverbal, timeless manner, in which one realizes that the Self is eternal. It has no beginning, it has no ending, and that which I am, has always been, and will always be.

What we do in life is we try to transcend the self with a small s—the selfishness, self-centeredness, greed, hatred, anger, all the negative emotions associated with it—and allow and facilitate the growth of the Self with a capital S because that is infinitely gratifying.

As we see from the calibrated levels of consciousness, the higher the level of consciousness, the more you're dominated by the Self, with the capital S, rather than the self with the small s, and the greater your happiness is. When you don't need fancy titles and money and all these other things, then you're no longer run by them, and you begin to value other things. You're able to love everyone, no matter what. I can look at people in the current political scene that I disagree with completely and still love them as fellow human beings.

You allow yourself to love everyone equally. As your consciousness advances, you can see what motivates people—it becomes very transparent; and the funny thing is, often what they say and the impression they're trying to make is in direct contrast to what they are really up to. It gets increasingly harder to deceive a person who is relatively enlightened.

Advanced states of consciousness often occur spontaneously. You're walking through the woods and suddenly you stop and realize the beauty of the trees and the birds singing. The intrinsic beauty of nature shines forth. If you're fortunate, you see the sacredness of it—you see that all existence is sacred. Each tree is conscious and aware of your presence, and realizes that God is walking by. It's aware of this on a certain level; it's aware on the vegetative level but there *is* the knowingness of it, because the infinite knowingness of divinity is intrinsic with all that exists.

The House of Mirrors

Humanity right now seems to be lost in the house of mirrors, unable to tell the difference between reality and illusions. Lights are shown on different mirrors and people think that what they are seeing is real, when it is merely the reflection in the mirror.

More than half of the people in the United States calibrate below level 200. Levels below 200 come from force and are destructive to life, and levels above 200 come from power. As we humans evolved, we started at the bottom and gradually moved up. This is the level where we have evolved up to this particular point. The levels 200 and up represent truth and integrity, and the levels below 200 are in falsehood.

Simply put, the way to stay above 200 is to follow the Ten Commandments and avoid the seven deadly sins. You avoid craving, wanting, desiring, and demanding. You give up pride and the narcissism that it's based on. You give up resentments and angers. You give up being fearful.

When we're calibrating levels of consciousness, what we are doing is getting to the essence of a thing, not its appearance.

In an infinite timeless space, there is no beginning or end, there is no here or there, there is no now or then. Consequently, the field of consciousness is omniscient by virtue of being all that has ever been or can be. So when we find the essence, what happens is we collapse the wave function.

In quantum mechanics, we have the Heisenberg principle. You go from the trading and equations of the possible, time dependent or time independent. Then the wave function—which is really a mathematical formula—potentiates, and you can collapse the wave function, meaning you go from energy to particle. It was discovered, of course, in trying to research the basic nature of light itself; it occurs in waves of particles. Therefore, the potential becomes an actual only if there is a reality.

If I make a statement that has a reality to it, this affects the quantum potential and collapses the wave function, and the person's arm goes strong. If I pose a question that is false, it has no corollary in reality, therefore it has no power and it does not collapse the wave function, and their arm goes weak. This is muscle testing in action.

In today's world, about 80 percent of the world's population is below 200. When you're talking about truth and integrity and honesty, most of the world has no clue what that is.

Life originates from top down, from the radiance of divinity, shining forth through the power of the field of consciousness, which then emerges as life—and a whole range of choices. This range of choices is determined by your level of consciousness. Often when we pray to God for guidance, what happens is a good idea pops into our head but we don't see that's the consequence of our asking for help and respecting divinity. Funnily, this act invokes divinity.

The same applies to truth. If your desire is to comprehend and become aware of truth and be led to truth, then the likelihood is that is exactly what's going to happen. Those who refute God and refute truth pay the consequence. They can't use the simple muscle test for truth that we have found so useful in hundreds of different areas. If you deny that there is such a thing as truth or the source of truth, then you're denied the gifts that ensue from that belief. How you view and experience the world is a projection, and it's a projection of your own consciousness out there and to what you believe to be out there. There isn't any out there, there's only an "in here."

Can you see the world, as I described, as a place of maximum karmic benefit? What you see and experience is a projection of your own consciousness—viewing the world as sad, happy, ludicrous, beneficial, beautiful, divine, frustrating, corrupt, evil, or an infinite good. If we want to reach advanced states of enlightenment and realize the ultimate divinity, we must grow into that dimension of awareness. The karmic benefit of human lifetime, as the Buddhist said, would be self-rewarding.

In America today, about 1 in 10 million people place becoming enlightened at the top of their ambitions, so this pursuit is very rare, but incredibly rewarding.

To facilitate your spiritual evolution, surround yourself with beauty: art, music, dance, literature. Beauty has a direct physical influence on the neurons in the brain. Those neurons are favorably influenced and energize the side of your brain that produces endorphins.

Of course, in spiritual evolution, you eventually transcend any definition of beauty because you begin to now sense the beauty of all of existence, and you can walk down an alley and be stunned by what you see. I remember this one time I walked down an alleyway in New York City and, all of a sudden, everything was illuminated. The rusted garbage cans were a work of art. A little brown mouse scurried by looking for food and found an apple. It made me so happy. The whole thing looked like an Impressionistic painting.

Appreciating art and creativity can enhance your spiritual awareness. Great works of art—music, theater, dance—can make us cry. Its beauty reaches a certain point, and we cannot help but break out in tears of joy and bliss. We're transported to a state of ecstasy.

Going Deeper into the House of Mirrors

My concern about the impact of the media in today's world, the degree to which people are totally brainwashed, is that this eventually leads to dissolution and lowering of the level of consciousness. The decline of morality has been speeded up by the media. Young children are so impressionable, and they're being so completely overtaken by the media that they almost become puppets of the media.

The awareness itself is sufficient protection. The decline of our own society is caused by a lack of respect and a lack of understanding of the necessity for sovereignty. Sovereignty is not popular in today's world. People don't understand sovereignty—because the ultimate sovereignty is divinity. The adolescent within us doesn't want to have to deal with sovereignty; it wants to have its own narcissistic playful, good time and do what it wants to do in self-indulgence.

Now, sovereignty means that it's aligned with absolutism rather than relativism. True sovereignty has no interest in what people's opinion is about it, it just is. You see it for what it is and each thing is serving its own purpose at that moment. It's funny, depending on if you think it's funny. It's sad, if you think it's sad. It's pathetic, it's outrageous, it's evil, it's good. All those things are things we project onto it.

The value of calibrating levels of consciousness is that it allows you to define and identify the essence of the thing versus its *perception*. That of course is going to be a big part of the house of mirrors.

Here, we're going to dive deeper and take a cruise through the entire totality of the human experience. The first thing that we begin to ask about the reality of being a human being is: How do we know what we are and where we came from? From the mammalian viewpoint, we know where we came from evolutionarily, but that is different than being human. What makes us human is the spirit and the etheric body.

How did we get here? The answer is quite a bit different depending on who you ask. The materialist is very happy with an animal evolution, is very happy with a linear, Newtonian explanation, from the bottom up. It means quite a different thing to a spiritual person. The creationist says God created man from the top down.

In advanced states of spirituality, you realize that you're not just a physicality, you have consciousness and awareness, and you came from top down, not from bottom up.

The explanation from the book of Genesis, that says man was created by God, calibrates at 1,000. We were created by an act of special creation—every one of us then is a child of God. Everyone here is a child of God. Therefore, everyone out there is our brother or our sister.

Where did we come from? Who are we? Are we body, or are we spirit? We're a spiritualized body. We see the difference in brain function, of left brain versus right brain, as the effect of the spiritual energy. The spiritual energy then lights up the levels of awareness, the spiritual as person. So the minute you become spiritually committed, you pray to God and say, "Dear God, I ask you to help me. I ask for your will for me." You've already brought up an energy that now enables you to understand the answer. You finesse a whole field of awareness and become much empowered as a human being when you realize that you're a spiritualized body, not just a physical body.

Where do we go? We transform into a different energy field. Your etheric body now becomes your primary body.

Why are we in this world? That would of course depend on what is the purpose of life. The purpose of human life has been debated in all the great books of the

Western world. The answer is, we're not. You're not in this world. The world is in you. Why? Because it's only your consciousness that is even aware of the world.

Going back to our purpose, it seems obvious from just looking at history that our purpose is to support the evolution of our consciousness. This world gives us the maximum opportunity to grow and develop spiritually.

Everybody has a perception. The basic dictum about that was presented in the dialogue between Protagoras and Plato. "I experience the world in one way and you experience it in another way, so there's two different realities," he says. The perception is not reality, however; how you perceive the world is your opinion, but that's not necessarily how the world is. You don't live in two different realities; you live in two different *perceptions* of reality. They're not different realities; they're different points of perception. What you perceive out there is a projection of what you are.

There are many different ways of viewing the world. Is it a comedy? Is it a tragedy? The naive person only sees perception. The more advanced person is interested in the actual essence of a thing—its absolute truth. Life is too short to throw away your time and energy and commitment on fallacious, fly-by-night enthusiasms.

Our society is great at drumming up enthusiasm for the latest catastrophe. What you're talking about is a narcissistic investment, which is really a whole other subject, but of great importance. It isn't so much your opinion or your view or what you stand for, but the degree to which you have a narcissistic investment in it. The minute a thing gets to be an "ism," as soon as you put I-S-M on the end of a viewpoint, it drops in calibration to about 180 or 190. The minute it becomes an ism, then you have the protests, the marches, the division. People who don't agree with you become your enemy. They're not really interested in knowing the truth; they just want you to echo their beliefs.

Obstacles to Raising One's Level of Consciousness

Consciousness levels below 200 are antitruth. They're only interested in their own view of the world and justifying it. But as you become more evolved, you become detached; you don't invest your emotions in being right or wrong.

Most people, when they use muscle testing, are unable to detach. They have such an investment in the outcome that they preclude getting to the truth. I always tell people to first detach. They must find out what they're looking for, what they calibrate at, and then adjust to that later. So if somebody you think is a lying, cheating rat turns out to calibrate high, first find out what they calibrate on, then think about why you saw them that way and adjust your feeling about it. Don't do it in reverse.

Many people are so narcissistic that they cannot put their own preferences aside long enough to find out what the truth is. You can't really calibrate levels of truth if your own consciousness is below 200. In fact, the higher it is, the greater the accuracy. This research was conducted by colleagues of ours who found that the higher the level of consciousness, the greater the percentage of truthfulness of the response to the muscle test. The best range

is in the 400s. The 400s is the level of intellect, truth, and logic. A person who's in the 400s is more likely to be motivated to understand the truth. They're less driven by ego and emotion.

If you're a scientist doing an experiment, this is not the place for emotion. "I want these bacteria to be gram positive instead of gram negative!" Sounds absurd, doesn't it? The trained person has learned how to ignore emotion and find out through logic.

So truth is one thing, and the position that people take about the truth is another. You can disagree with it, but that has nothing to do with the truth. Let's say you bought a certain stock, and it went down. It wasn't right—it was supposed to go up!

The absolute says that there is a reality that is beyond subjectivity. To the relativist, the idea that there's a truth beyond your person ego is an anathema, because the relativist is based on narcissism. As you get more evolved, the conscience becomes more predominant and you can't fool yourself or others anymore. Up to a certain point, lying doesn't bother you as long as you have a gain, but then lying starts to bother you. You eventually reach a point where lying to yourself is an anathema. You might still be right to lie to others, but you're not going to lie to yourself.

Quieting the Mind with Meditation and Contemplation

Meditation serves a powerful purpose because of the intention and discipline we bring to it. Meditation also consumes our time and space. Contemplation, on the other hand, is more a way of being in the world and experiencing openness. Meditation takes you out of the world. You can't be playing with the kids or mowing the lawn, so meditation is a formal discipline.

Contemplation is a sort of a semimeditated state. You watch everything from a somewhat detached state because you become the witness instead of the subject of phenomena. It takes you out of the field, so you're no longer the star of what's happening.

As time goes back and you practice contemplation more regularly, it becomes obvious to you one day that all sorts of phenomena occur spontaneously on their own. There is no personal *I* causing anything to happen. Because you feel and see the arm moving through the air, you presume that *I* decided to move the arm through the air. You take credit for it—in one 10,000th of a second—that's how fast the narcissistic ego jumps in. The personal, *I*, takes many lifetimes to finally dissolve and you become the nonlinear, all-prevailing witness of the phenomena and the identity of who you are moves to the witness, to the experiencer, to the field of consciousness itself. And then it moves to that capacity for awareness *within* consciousness itself.

Let's say we're sitting here right now. Well, for us to sit here, we have to get born. For us to get born, we have parents. There are millions of options that would've had to have taken place. Millions of phenomena have to occur to account for even the smallest event—a piece of dust going through the air.

People ask, "What is the cause of this little piece of dust floating in front of my eyes?" There are millions of factors to account for why this piece of dust, right now in this room, is moving at this rate of speed, under this

atmospheric pressure and wind speed, under these temperatures, and so on. It's not possible for the human mind to discern the actual true cause of a thing. So eventually you surrender, you find your humility in all of existence.

By becoming the witness, the phenomena are obviously occurring of their own accord. This becomes obvious after a while. This is a realization where you transcend the identification with the personal self, and this can come out of contemplation. Meditation may intensify it, but what often happens is meditation gets separated from daily life. There's meditation, and then there's daily life. Contemplation brings about a meditative, inner lifestyle that you can practice all the time, everywhere, anytime. In a way, contemplation is more like vision. You witness what is out there. You don't cause it, you don't take personal credit. When you are in this state of witnessing, you are closer to your real self.

Many spiritual pathways give you a lesson for the day, such as an affirmation or verse to reflect on. This gives you one thing that you play with in your mind all day, something that you hold lightly in your mind.

I remember when I did this with the 91st Psalm. "He that dwelleth in the secret place of the Most High shall abide under the shadow of the Almighty." I spent hours and hours just looking at that verse. Its true meaning comes forth in different levels of comprehension and understanding, and that occurs spontaneously.

After doing this for a while, you learn how to be with what's happening around you while maintaining a contemplative awareness. You're aware that you're hustling and bustling, but the real you is not really hustling and bustling—the real you is *witnessing* the hustling and bustling. Of course, you know the mind thinks it must get all this done, and you can laugh at the mind and say, *Mind, sit down a second. I know you feel you must get this all done by 10:00 or else the world will come to an end.* You learn how to joke with yourself.

I find that with these spiritual tools and techniques, a sense of humor is key. It keeps you from getting so dreadfully serious about yourself and so self-opinionated. It helps you avoid the narcissism of wanting to be right. A sense of humor gives you a certain perspective, with an emphasis on reality and detachment. As a person becomes more spiritually aware, life becomes more lighthearted and less serious, even humorous at times. Being able to laugh at oneself in a loving manner is a definite blessing along the way.

——

CHAPTER 2

How to Fit In While Remaining Conscious

There is a perception that as one becomes more enlightened, it is harder to live in the world. In this chapter, Dr. Hawkins will provide hope and encouragement about walking a spiritual path in this world and explain how awakening actually brings a greater ease into the experience.

He will focus on how to best live consciously in a predominantly unconscious world. To begin, Dr. Hawkins discusses the dangers of the herd instinct, or "groupthink." He explores why people will do things in a crowd that they would not even think about doing alone. How is the herd instinct showing up in today's world, and how can we avoid getting pulled in?

The herd instinct phenomenon is what the media plays on and what they try to propagate. It usually starts with a leader, someone who stands up and tries to rally the troops and get everyone cheering. This person is the energizer; that's their function. We can use consciousness calibration to find out if their cause is worthy. Is what they're energized about based in truth, or is it all an illusion? Illusion will excite the crowd just as much as truth, after all.

The competition in today's world is for moral superiority. That's the basis of all the major conflicts going on. If you watch the news from that viewpoint, you'll be amused. You will see this constant, narcissistic drive for moral superiority. People's affiliations and causes—their religion, their political party, their nationality, even their generational identity—become more about how they are perceived than anything else, and this is used to pit various groups against each other.

True Spiritual Leadership

How do we rise above this division? In order to lead, we encourage greater and greater independence, and not just reliance on the teacher. You begin to strive for excellence, for the sake of excellence. Excellence is its own reward.

A sense of moral responsibility is probably the best guide—moral responsibility toward yourself, others, and God. As I mentioned, moral superiority is the narcissistic drive of the ego to put someone else down in order to feel superior, whereas moral responsibility is being the best one can be toward yourself, others, and God. You're serving God, your Self with a capital S, and your fellow man. And in doing any one of them, you're also doing the other two.

I can remember all the years I had a huge practice and the demand I put upon myself was to do my utmost for my patient. Am I being true to myself, and do I want to be answerable for this decision at some later date?

I started to get into really innovative treatments. I treated many hopeless cases. And very often I found answers to the unanswerable and cures for the incurable. And still, my colleagues would ridicule me. Even now, if I speak to a group of conventional, Western-trained physicians about acupuncture, they'll roll their eyes. Well, my own personal experience with acupuncture was this: years ago, I had an intractable, perforating ulcer that frequently bled and put me in the hospital. I was scheduled for a gastric resection—a surgical removal of the stomach—which was very risky given the condition I was in in those days.

As luck would have it, the first acupuncture clinic soon opened in Washington, D.C. It was approved by the federal government. It was experimental and therefore everything was carefully documented. You had to get a referral from your doctor. After my third treatment, this intractable, incurable disease was cured. I have never in all of the years since then had a recurrence of the ulcer. So I truly think your intention and your mindset has something to do with it.

Everything you desire is something you project outside yourself. Whatever it is that you're projecting—your desires, your frustrations—is all due to the fact that you've projected the reality of who you really are to something or someone out in the outer world and have assigned it to some quality. And when you own the reality of that, which you are, you realize that you, your Self, is whole and complete within itself. Your Self needs nothing. Therefore, nobody has anything that you want out there because you're sufficient, and whole, and complete from moment to moment.

Discovering Self-Approval and Self-Acceptance

As you progress along the spiritual path, you begin to see that you are sufficient unto yourself and are answerable only to yourself. The question becomes simple: Am I fulfilling my greatest capacity to God, to myself, to my fellow man, and to those I love? Your obligation to divinity is to be all that you can be to yourself, to God, and to everyone. In this way, you are fulfilling your promise. Therefore, what could approval do for you? Approval doesn't do anything but build up your ego. If you're lacking nothing, that approval is unnecessary. If you've done the best you can, you don't need other people's approval.

It's sort of like getting a hole-in-one on the golf course. It just falls in the cup by accident. It's exciting, but it's not really a skill because if it was a skill, you'd be able to do it a second time.

What is the purpose of human life, then? It facilitates the evolution of consciousness to the realization of our ultimate reality. It's a part of the pathway to enlightenment. The question then arises, how did this world arise? It depends on what you mean by this world—the planet, our humanity, the human experience? The world that we're talking about is a state of consciousness. This world arose as a karmic benefit, as an automatic consequence of what we have become. Intrinsic to the human experience, so prominent in today's world, is the birth of morality.

Our morality, our sense of right and wrong, is innate, wired into the nervous system. And over time, a society will go through periods of great confusion and collapse because the definitions of morality, of what's right, what's wrong, what's real, what's not real, radically changes.

Not only is it constantly changing, it changes with the decade, it changes with the media, but it also changes throughout an individual's life. What's right and wrong in infancy is not the same in childhood, in adolescence, in adulthood, in middle age, and even in old age.

A shared agreement on all of these matters brings about social accord and enables governance. Without agreement, there's discord. And what changes the whole picture, once you think you've got this all down pat, then comes politicization. All the definitions of right and wrong, what's moral, what's appropriate are now edited. Politicization is a way of constantly editing everything.

Everything has become politicized. The language, the words, every inflection and gesture is now politicized. And you have to be careful how you phrase things, because if you use one wrong word, that's it.

You can see how complex trying to understand human behavior is now. We're piling mirrors upon mirrors upon mirrors. The realization is that you are not limited by this world or even *definable* by this world. Your spirit, your Self, is not measurable by this world, and it's not visible to this world. So you want to transcend the world—to be in it, but not of it, not limited by it. To be limited by it is to buy all of its programs. To buy all of its programs, you're going to have to run around and buy everything that's for sale, because if you're successful, you'll have those things. You can't possibly meet all the definitions of success, though, because you should have more friends, you should be more attractive, you should have more money. There's always something you can find fault with about yourself, and you'll never be satisfied.

The secret is to be happy with what you are at the moment, and also see that you're an evolving human being. Therefore, you don't have to be perfect because you're not required to be perfect. You're only expected to make the best possible use you can of the advantages you have to learn and to grow, to support others, and to be loving and forgiving. Then you're doing all you can do as a human being.

The Power of Gratitude

Gratitude gives us an opportunity to better understand and experience negative circumstances. Here's an example I like to use from real life: If somebody backs into my car in the parking lot, I'm always concerned with making the other person feel better. I tell them, "Don't worry about it. It happens to everybody. You have insurance. I have insurance. It's no big deal." It's just a nuisance, really. It's nothing to ruin your life or someone else's life.

I find that making other people feel happy is in itself very gratifying, because you can see the person's worries slowly vanish and their relief is palpable. They go from thinking that you're going to sue them to a place of calm and peace. You get to reassure them that all is well. It's a wonderful thing to make someone feel better, instead of intensifying a stressful situation.

Soon, you'll learn that this way of life is extremely pleasant and you're surrounded by friendly, loving people, and that you feel good when you go to bed at night. Your life becomes gratifying and your happiness is radiated out into the world. By being this way, you become like a relay station for higher levels of consciousness to utilize you as a pathway to others.

The Paradigms of Science and Spirituality

Science is in a paradigm of the linear, logical, and causality, and it calibrates in the 400s. This exists in the Newtonian paradigm of reality, which includes ordinary physics, mathematics, science, and reason. The spiritual paradigm, however, is a different paradigm, and it calibrates 500 and up.

Therefore, science is more limited. Spiritual reality calibrates from 500 and up, so you find that you cannot prove love. You cannot prove it, because it's a nonlinear, ineffable thing—to be in love or to love something. You cannot prove love scientifically, but it's powerful. A person will give up everything in this world and walk to the ends of the earth for love.

Love is of a different dimension and a different quality. The same goes for beauty—music, the arts. You can't take the temperature of music. Music doesn't have a temperature. Temperature is of one domain and music is of another. Thus, you can't prove or disprove spiritual reality using science. The only thing I know, the thing that crosses the bridge somewhat, is what I call clinical. Academic science cannot cross the bridge. Clinical science

can certainly bring likelihoods and inferences, but it cannot bring proof.

We've conducted calibrations over the years and have gained a lot of information about these ineffable states. It has helped us understand and determine likelihoods, but it is not a certainty. It's not proof in the scientific sense. Spiritual reality is not the world of proofs. You can prove things within the linear dimension, the calibrated levels of the 400s. You cannot prove anything from 500 and up.

What is proof to one man? What is certitude to another man? A doubting Thomas will doubt anything right up to the point of divinity. Skepticism is its own limitation, and it calibrates at around 170. It is a negative state of mind, and it invalidates anything that is not pedestrian and obvious. It misses all the mystery of life, the essence of things.

When you see the world the way it is, it's not a product of doubt. Do you doubt that music at the symphony is beautiful? No. I just felt a chill go up the back of my neck. It's not a mentalization or a judgment. There are certain pieces in the opera that literally send a chill right up the back of your spine. You cannot discredit that. The music is so stunningly beautiful, so astonishing, and there's no scientific way to prove that.

Maintaining Childlike
Innocence and Wonder

Children are innocent because they have not yet been programmed. However, as we age, our intrinsic innocence still remains within; therefore, through spiritual evolution, we reach the point called discernment. Discernment is classically called the opening of the third eye of the Buddhic body.

It occurs at a consciousness level of 600s. This is also known as Sat-Chit-Ananda in Hindu philosophy. At this level, you can leave the world or stay in the world—it makes no difference. With the opening of the third eye of the Buddhic body, one intrinsically has the capacity to discern the essence of a thing. You see through the sheep's clothing, and you notice the wolf there.

So once the third eye of the Buddhic body opens, you realize that inside the sheep's clothing there's a wolf waiting to kill you—not literally. They're going to instill their opinions and values into you, the child. You will then adopt, incorporate, identify with these standards, norms, and ethics to the extent that it becomes hardwired—your programming.

So the way to change that programming is to be yourself. It's not easy when we are lost in a house of mirrors. At every turn then, we begin to see things differently. At every turn, you can see how complex human life is. One thing we can do is honor this complex, ever-shifting human life. It takes a huge amount of will and devotion to life to just keep walking on with your head held high. The levels of consciousness, as we know, are karmic propensities. Some of them are gifts of God. And the purpose of human life is really the evolution of consciousness.

As we age, we have to constantly change our expectations of ourselves and others, our social roles. We're constantly shifting our understanding of the interaction of this enormous complexity.

If you look at life, you can see we have an endless array of decisions from each second to the next. You can either go in this direction or that one. Each choice leads to another one. If we calibrate every decision and always follow the yes answer—which is the higher consciousness level—we will end up in a completely different flow than a person who always chooses the no. Following truth will ultimately take you to God.

Achieving Infinite, Timeless Bliss

So by constantly following truth, you will eventually end up at God, and at certain levels of consciousness, like joy and ecstasy. Joy and ecstasy are incapacitating, and you cannot function. The joy is exquisite. The ecstasy is indescribable. The ecstasy of the first exposure to the energy field of God—divinity directly—fills one with exquisite joy beyond all time, and beyond all expression.

So the knowingness that came to me was that this too must be surrendered to God, the state of ecstasy. And I surrendered ecstasy. I can't tell you how captivating it is. It was not all that easy. But then I realized that this too must be surrendered, so I knelt down and I surrendered the ecstasy. And then came a piece beyond all description. Infinite, unending, foreverness, the feeling of completion, total completion. And at that point you have permission to leave the body. You don't need to stay with the body. You're not obligated to stay with it or leave it.

You're free to leave because that which you are is not the body, and whether it survives or not is irrelevant. Whether it survives or not is really up to the karma of the world and the karma of the people in your life. You surrender yourself to the will of God or whatever the energy field is that is being experienced—infinite, timeless bliss. And what happens after that is up to God's will.

——

CHAPTER 3

How the Law of Attraction Fits Into Your Spiritual Journey

In this chapter, Dr. Hawkins will offer his insights regarding the Law of Attraction. He will explain what is at the root of the Law of Attraction and suggest an even more powerful method that you can utilize in your daily life: the Law of Intention. Dr. Hawkins will also reveal why people become obsessed with the latest spiritual fad, and how we can best work with the knowledge we can gain through the calibration process to assist us along our spiritual path in an integrous and congruent manner.

‑‑

In spiritual work, the key understanding is that what you hold in mind tends to manifest. This is very practical; instead of using willpower, what we're doing is holding a vision of what's desirable, and this tends to manifest. The explanation scientifically is really based on quantum mechanics. The potential of the universe is calculated via the Schrödinger process, and that denotes the possibilities. The next thing that is invoked is intention. What it does is it triggers the Heisenberg principle of intention. An intention collapses the wave function of the potential to the actual. That's how the kinesiologic test works also. And that's the Heisenberg process.

The Heisenberg process introduces the effect of consciousness and intention. And if there's a possibility then that's doable, you might say, what happens is the Dirac process—where you collapse the wave function from the potential to the actual. So for instance, throughout my life, I've held in my mind where I wanted to live. If I wanted a little house by the creek, I had a little house by the creek. Whatever it is I wanted, that's what materialized.

This is not magic. The Law of Intention is based in quantum mechanics: the potential becomes the actual when local conditions facilitate it. Intention increases the likelihood of manifesting what is being held in the mind. This has been around throughout my entire lifetime.

When you utilize the power of intention, what you're taking advantage of is the power of the field of consciousness itself. Consciousness is beyond time and dimension and location, and it is also without limitation. So the possible becomes the actual, and what determines that is when local conditions are favorable. When local conditions are favorable, then the potential actualizes as the actual.

It's been phrased somewhat differently by other experts. Rupert Sheldrake is a biologist and researcher in the field of consciousness, and his principle [is] essentially the same—that what you hold in mind tends to manifest when local conditions are favorable. He [calls] it formative causation. This principle has been redescribed over the centuries from different viewpoints. Traditionally, it's been a prayer. When you pray, you're holding something in mind, and you're adding your intention to it. This begins the likelihood that this is going to manifest; it determines when it's going to become experiential in the physical world.

There's no limit to what you can manifest in the world. However, you don't know how many lifetimes you're affecting. What you're holding in mind and intensely desiring and praying for may not show up in this lifetime. The fact that something wonderful happens to you or something horrible happens to you is very often a likely hangover from a previous lifetime in which you were very intense about what you'd asked for. If you use consciousness testing and ask, "Is karma a legitimate actuality?" we always get a "Yes, it is." Even the Old Testament certainly says that the problems of mankind are karmic inheritance from having disobeyed God and eaten of the apple. Now, if that isn't karma, I don't know what is.

Calibrating the Law of Attraction

The Law of Attraction calibrates somewhere around 250. The fact that you're more likely to experience the thing doesn't mean it was attracted to you. Attraction is more like a big magnet, and you're not going to magically pull in these things from the universe. Intention increases the likelihood of what is held in the mind—it's what propels you to something, and not the other way around.

The 400s are really the domain of reason, and the 300s are more in the realm of feeling—enthusiasm, excitement. These feelings are great, but you're still left with the problem of how you're going to actually do it. We have lots of visionaries of ends and hardly any visionaries of means. Everybody wants to unify us all into one great big happy family. That's a great vision, but how do you *do* that? One thing you can do is look at all the scientific discoveries that have so benefited mankind. They all came out of science, and many of them occurred right in my lifetime. Doctors treated hopeless cases of syphilis, and then penicillin was invented, and with just one shot, was the cure. These are no doubt miracles. Many diseases were cured one after another with intention. It is with intention that we draw in the means and the mechanics involved.

Another factor to consider is the calibration level at which you are and exist. If a person calibrates quite high and holds something in mind, its likelihood of manifesting is sometimes close to 100 percent. People with a low negative calibration probably tend to manifest what they don't want.

The Power of the Present Moment

Think about this for a moment: if you live in the exact moment of *now*, you don't have any problems. I like to use the example of a person who is about to get beheaded. He's walking up to the scaffold, and at that moment, he has no problems. He steps on the stairs, and at that moment, still no problems. And then he places his head on the block—at that moment, he still doesn't have any problems.

If you're living in the moment, nothing's happening. And then wop, off goes your head, and guess what? You still don't have a problem! Even in the worst scenario, if you live in the instant of the exact moment of now, you see the creation of anxiety and negative feelings is based on projecting into the future. The anxiety and fear and disappointment is about the future or the past. If you watch your mind, you'll see you're usually either regretting something from the past or you're fearfully anticipating something in the future.

It used to be said, "Keep your mind where your body is," meaning in the exact moment of now. The average person is worrying about the future or hanging on to the past. For the future, you're going to anticipate positive responses, but also you anticipate fear.

Beginners in spiritual consciousness research tend to get confused because they mix consciousness levels. What's meant in one context cannot be criticized from another context. You can't contradict a statement from a different level of consciousness any more than you can criticize theology from the viewpoint of science. They are different paradigms. Science is a paradigm, and spiritual reality is a different paradigm. You can't criticize mathematics from the viewpoint of spirituality. That's mixing levels. For instance, a person might say, "Well, yes, I'm living in the now when I worry; I'm worrying right now. I'm living in the present when I regret the past; I'm regretting the past right now. So if I live in the right now, I've got regret over the past and anxiety about the future.

Then that's what I'm worried about right now. And that's my now, my now is full of anxiety and regrets."

Then they say, "Well, to get rid of regret and anticipatory fear, I need to get out of the now. By tomorrow, I'll have figured it all out." This is also denoting time. Just because you're paying attention to something doesn't make it the now. A contemplative lifestyle, which we talked about in Chapter 1, can help take you out of the ambiguity about now and not now and the future and the past; because when seen from the viewpoint of the witness of consciousness itself, there isn't any now, there isn't any past, there isn't any future.

Phenomena are unfolding, but they're not unfolding within a linear time track. There isn't a time track within consciousness. In consciousness, all things are equally present all the time because it's beyond time. There is no place within the infinite field of consciousness because it's infinite. Every place within the infinite universe is here right now, and all of time is available right now. And we can demonstrate that with consciousness calibration. We can calibrate what Cleopatra felt and thought and what she calibrated. People might say, "Well, that was in the past." No, it's now. Cleopatra's not in the past, nothing is in the past. Everything is now, and everything is here. The reason is that within consciousness everything is recorded forever. Everything that ever happened is

41

recorded forever, and it's not filed according to past, present, or future—it's all present right now. Everything that ever happened is equally present right now, right here.

In an infinite universe, where is the center? The center of an infinite universe is everywhere. In an infinite time, when is now? Now is all time. So these are different levels of abstraction, and in the enlightened state, no such problem would be mentalized because it's not seen as a problem. There's only the awareness of awareness of awareness. I think of it more in terms of aesthetics and shifting your brain function from left-brain, linear, logical, sequential, volitional thinking to more right-brain appreciation. When you're walking through the beautiful woods and you can hear the birds singing and the beautiful flowers from the spring, you're not thinking with your left brain. You're just into appreciation, aesthetics. The understanding of spiritual realities is increased by aesthetics.

Beautiful music, dance, paintings, cathedrals—beauty is intrinsic to celebrating divinity. I remember looking at a carving of a pulpit that was a couple stories high. It took the carver an entire lifetime to carve this pulpit. He spent his entire life carving this. And what's impressive about the great cathedrals is that hundreds and hundreds of men spent their entire lifetimes on them for over a century.

These magnificent buildings—Westminster Abbey, Notre-Dame, Chartres Cathedral—bring you down to humility. You become aware that you are such a small little entity, that you will never be noticed within these massive architectural achievements. You experience an appreciation for the greatness of mankind, to hold in mind Westminster Abbey and spend a thousand years constructing it. Lifetime after lifetime, people sacrifice their lives for beauty, for elaborate carvings and great stained glass windows that can never be reproduced.

You can disappear time. And of course, when you are in great moments of your life, time disappears. In fact, the experience of time is really resistance to experiencing. And when you stop resisting experiencing and allow experiencing to experience itself, the sense of time disappears. I learned that from a practical viewpoint, because it used to be very boring to drive from Phoenix to where I live. I started to use my mind to disappear time, and as soon as I did that, I would notice I would leave Phoenix and I was home already—disappeared the entire trip, several boring hours on the road gone.

It's impossible for half of the population to comprehend spiritual reality; it's impossible. Why? They can only understand the linear domain, the Newtonian world of causality. They have no comprehension of the nonlinear. They don't understand context. And the best example of

43

context influencing morality is situational ethics. People say, "Well, no, no. What's right and wrong is absolute." It all depends on the context. Every courtroom case is a case of context. "What happened before you pulled the trigger? Were you being threatened?" "I thought I was being threatened, but it wasn't really a gun. It was only hamburger he was trying to get out of his pocket." We always look at the context. What was the intention?

We cannot predict the future, because the future is the product of intention of decisions along the way. You and I right now are deciding the future. So how could the future know what's going to be until our time together is over? The present is based on decisions and intentions and choices being made now. So creation and evolution are one and the same thing. Without that background, you wouldn't understand what I'm saying. Creation, divinity ordained that creation was evolutionary. And if you look over the history of all of life, you see it's all evolutionary. From the simple, single-cell bacteria to the complex human, the consciousness level of life over time constantly advances.

The reason you can't predict the future is because the determinants of the future have not occurred yet. And the future will be determined by decisions that are made by millions of people who haven't made them yet. A deterministic outcome would be fatalism, and fatalism calibrates low. So because the human is evolutionary, because our consciousness is evolutionary, the factors that determine future events have not occurred yet because these are options of the human will. Therefore, if collectively, we all think in a certain way, then a likelihood is going to occur, but not a certainty. You're still not going to determine the future.

Man's power as compared to the infinite power of the universe and the field of consciousness, which is omnipotent, is picayune. Within one cubic centimeter of space, there is more energy in that one cubic centimeter of space, more power in that than its equivalent in the total mass of the universe.

Therefore, a very powerful entity who holds something in mind is going to increase the likelihood more than somebody who is at a less powerful level of consciousness.

As a young man, I was once invited to join a prestigious society, and I declined. Intuitively, I knew not to. I declined because I found you had to take a sacred vow and that vow was phrased: "If I ever violate this, may the opposite be my fate." And that's binding through many, many lifetimes.

So that's the whole basis of the research technique we use—to show that a person who's highly evolved won't respond to a minor negative energy, but a person who is not so evolved will respond to it easily. That's why you see these cults gain momentum. The people who join them calibrate under 200.

The Strength of Spiritually Evolved People

Let's say you get angry. If you've repressed a lot of anger over many lifetimes, you usually have a lot of residual anger. You're not going to get over that quickly by just forgiving your cat for chewing up your sock. You're accelerating the emergence into consciousness of things that are repressed, as well as the collective unconscious. So you're precipitating their processing. If you look at Encyclopædia Britannica, look under mystics; you'll notice that, classically, many of the most famous mystics of history live through prolonged periods of illness.

I did many lectures on health and healing, and I looked at things from my own lifetime. I experienced 26 diseases, half of which were practically fatal. Recurrent perforating ulcers, hemorrhagic diverticulitis, migraine headaches, and acute pancreatitis—just one thing after another—to the degree that I'm classified as a mystic now. A mystic is aware of an absolute truth without having to go through a process to reach it. They process it out using all the techniques they've learned. The fate of the body is of much less importance, I think, than to the average person. I faced the possibility of death, so I don't remember feeling any anxiety about that.

If you've ever had out-of-body experiences, you can actually see your own body laying over there. And the interesting thing is that the minute that you're out of body, you have no interest in the body.

The Impact of Community

A lot depends on how spiritually oriented a community is. A person who was intensely committed to spirituality would be understood in one setting and would be thought to be strange in another. Most mystics when they're around average, nonbelieving people, just don't stand out at all. When the mystic reaches a certain state of consciousness, they just abandon the whole world and take off, and then the world believes they've gone mad. What's happened is that a different reality has become predominant. The world of the ego and human ordinary consciousness is no longer valid—no longer motivates them. Money, success, and fame would be an aggravation. The mystic becomes committed to a different reality—aware of the infinite reality. And in the context of the presence of the Self with the capital *S*, the ambitions and fears and emotions of the self with the small s seem ridiculous. It seems rather absurd, but this is their life now.

You can't fake mysticism, either. You can't pretend that your ego doesn't still crave external, material gratification. You can't artificially dissolve it. It has to be a reality. And eventually, with spiritual effort, it becomes a reality and it is a dominant reality. So in the spiritual reality, the Self dominates the self and replaces it. One doesn't look to the self anymore because the overwhelming presence of the Self overpowers it. The fear of death disappears.

As we learned, people who are spiritually inclined often have had extensive exposure to music, the arts, and aesthetics. These things greatly influence brain function and neuronal connection. In my family, everybody was musical. My grandmother constantly played classical music when she was pregnant with my father, and people laughed at her and called her an ignorant old Irish lady. "You'll see," she said. And she was right. My father was a great musician. And then she used to read me Shakespeare. So classical music and Shakespeare, and then Saturday afternoon, the Metropolitan Opera would come on the radio from New York City, and Milton Cross would explain the opera. And pretty soon you're really caught up in the Nibelung Ring and looking forward to *Lohengrin*. It becomes intrinsic.

I've also touched on the importance of a sense of humor. I think this is extremely important, as important as any of the other things in life, like love and gratitude and solemnity. Humor has a healing effect among people. It points out the ambiguities in life, and it points out very often the ambiguity between the content and the context and how you sort of see the two end up really the opposite. Humor also has a way of connecting people and helping them put aside differences through a new perspective or mindset. People have written books on how they recovered from grave illnesses by just employing nothing but humor. Laughter releases endorphins in the brain and releases stress, among other major health benefits.

In today's world, the challenge is that because we're so hyperconnected through technology, we're constantly being indoctrinated and programmed through social media, through memes, quotes, and so on—phrases that become quoted so often that they're accepted as truth. They're accepted as truth just by sheer repetition.

Behind all of this and all of these things we've talked about is intention. It's all energized by intention. We must learn discernment—versus naively believing what we see. The human mind unaided is unable to tell truth from falsehood. The untrained mind is so dominated by the structure of the ego it cannot discern perception from essence. And one thing that brings up one's level of understanding of reality is narcissism versus spirituality.

The narcissistic mind is ruled by its own viewpoint, while the spiritual one seeks truth for its own sake. The antidote to narcissism is spirituality. Belief in God makes all the difference in the world, whether or not a person holds that God is a hypothetical likelihood. Skepticism is one thing, but atheism is another. I was a devout agnostic for many years. I was an atheist, but as I trained my brain, my thinking became more sophisticated, and I became an agnostic. The overall context in which this shift in understanding occurs is belief in God versus belief in no God. The house of mirrors looks completely different when it's illuminated by the light of divinity.

Calibrating Artists and Their Works

If you calibrate the great composers and great artists, they all calibrate quite high. Neurotic fears were not the source of their genius. You can look in the mirror and paint your own self-portrait and include in that the anguishes you've been through, but that is not the source of your genius; that's just the source of the subject matter. Take, for instance, Van Gogh's self-portrait, one of the most famous paintings in the world. Consider the overall calibration of the person in whom the phenomenon is occurring. You can be a creative genius and not share any of your anguish with the world. On the other hand, you may want to share that anguish. You can project it out there and let somebody else experience your inner anguish without identifying that it's yours in particular. Shakespeare was really a great writer. Surely, he expressed his personal experience of human anguish in his works, but because of the commonality of these experiences, they resonate with a wide variety of people. What Shakespeare expressed in his plays is still very, very pertinent in today's world.

The Power of Intention

I had a medical practice where a number of medical professionals worked: psychiatrists, therapists, social workers, and psychologists. I noticed that some of us had a higher rate of patient recovery than others, and I had a high degree of success with recovering patients. And sometimes I wondered, "What is the reason for that?" It has to do with intention—the willingness to do anything possible to help a patient recover. And I wasn't restricted by the routine scientific paradigm of reality. Traditional medicine calibrates around 440, but higher levels of medicine, which are more creative, calibrate 445 or 450. I intuitively learned that certain practices that other doctors deem alternative or unconventional would help certain patients. Consider acupuncture, for example. Traditional Chinese medicine is frowned upon by modern physicians. I almost died of recurrent hemorrhagic duodenal ulcers, and the doctors couldn't figure out a way to help. In three acupuncture treatments, I was cured. So how can you discredit something that cures you in three treatments—and the medical profession couldn't do it in 20 or 25 years?

Successful recovery requires open-mindedness and the willingness to explore beyond what are considered the normal avenues of treatment. Many medical professionals lack that willingness to think outside the realm of what are considered socially acceptable diagnoses and practices, which hinders their ability to help their patients recover.

I had a patient who suffered from [all kinds of symptoms]. He went through the routine procedures of treatment, seeing psychiatrists at Stanford and UCLA. Nearly 40 different psychiatrists attempted to treat him, but none of their methods were helpful methods. Not one of those psychiatrists was able to properly diagnose him or assist in his recovery.

When he showed up at my office, he had all but given up. It was obvious to me that the man needed my help. Since the standard psychiatric treatments did not solve his problems, I ordered a hair test, which is something else the medical profession frowns upon. It didn't come about as logic or reasoning; I listened to my mind. The results of the hair test revealed that the mercury levels in his body had reached toxic levels. We detoxed him from mercury using very high doses of vitamin C and ascorbic acid, and he completely recovered. Nobody could diagnose him, nor did they know how to treat him. None of that came about via the left-brain logic, but rather through an intuitive knowingness. It was obvious this man was suffering but didn't follow any functional pattern.

Patients often called me with reports of depression, anxiety and anxiety attacks, intense phobias, and sudden bouts of rage. I'd suggest they stop eating sugar until they come in for an appointment, and a quarter of them no longer would experience these symptoms by the time they saw me. One of the most misdiagnosed medical conditions is functional hypoglycemia. Medical professionals are quick to diagnose patients with these symptoms with ADHD or bipolar disorder without ruling out the possibility of functional hypoglycemia. In fact, low levels of blood glucose can lead to cerebral dysfunction and poor adrenal function, which can cause unpredictable changes in temperament and mood swings. By eliminating sugar, patients can eliminate anxiety attacks, insomnia, depression, and even sudden rages.

Final Thoughts on the Law of Attraction

An advanced teacher would tell you to forget the Law of Attraction, because that's just the ego's willfulness desiring a certain outcome, projecting it into the world, and chasing willows with success. You let go of all attractions and aversions. Instead of bemoaning the fact that you're not a millionaire, you give up the idea of being a millionaire. There is an illusion that being a millionaire is going to make you happy, but that is not necessarily the case. That desire satisfies that ambition for that moment, so you feel because that one is eliminated, that you're going to be okay. But if you don't change the habits of the ego, new issues will arise. The ego will just find a new way to take over. It's this whole idea that specialness projects specialness onto something. Research shows that people who win the lottery don't tend to see an improvement in their quality of life. Every negative outcome you can imagine befalls these people who suddenly win vast sums of money. The results can be devastating; we see increased rates of suicide, divorce, and addiction. There is a fantasy that millions of dollars will lead to happiness, but what it actually does is create a great deal of stress.

You remove the obstacles to spiritual reality, and it merges. When you're being dominated by the self with the small s, the ego's wants and desires and attractions and aversions, then it allows the Self with the capital S to radiate forth. Within the radiance of the Self with the capital S, there are no desires or aversions. Everything just is what it is. The advice of a more advanced teacher would be to stop projecting the energy field of glamor onto externals and stop projecting fears and attractions and aversions. The pristine state, then, is a state without attractions or aversions, and in that pristine state, everything merely is. And if everything merely is, then there's absolute peace. Look at where you are right at this moment: where the book is, where your feet are, what is around you. Everything just is. So what's the problem? There isn't a problem. You would have to create one in your mind. And then you project it into the world.

There's usually a period once you get spiritually oriented or spiritually interested in life where you're sort of karmically called forth or at least inspired by other people. Most people go through a period of research. They read a lot of books, they listen to a lot of lecturers, and they become attracted. There are karmic influences at play, so while they've forgotten why they're attracted to certain things, they will start becoming attracted. And somehow by holding in mind that you want an advanced teacher, you become conscious of your information about the availability of one. There's a period of searching for

the adequate teacher unless you have specifically in mind exactly what you want to begin with. In which case, you would then begin attending.

You attend the lectures by that particular teacher because you want your aura to pick up the energy field of the aura of that teacher. The teacher of advanced consciousness has a very powerful energy field in their aura, and you can calibrate the energy field of the teacher. What happens is that your aura picks up the frequency of the energy field of the teacher. This frequency of the energy field of the teacher may persist within the spiritual aura for many lifetimes. A person who becomes enlightened may have picked up the energy field of the great teacher 8 or 10 lifetimes ago, but now it's manifest. So traditionally, you visit the teacher, and many people study the teacher, meditate on the teacher's image, whatever reinforces the commitment and begins to advance to that level himself. The physicality is actually, unfortunately, a physicality of the experience of the aura of the teacher that transmits it.

When I went into what the world calls a very advanced state of consciousness, that came up in the form of knowingness, and with that knowingness was an absolute certainty. Faced with giving up the source of life itself, I'd given up everything in my world, every attraction, every aversion, and then there opened the awareness that I was still clinging to one thing. This too must be laid down before thee oh Lord, and that was life itself. The source of life itself, which you intuit at that level because everything else is removed, is stemming from within the ego itself. And so at that point I laid down my will about life, my will to be, the will to be in the form of life itself. I surrendered this too to thee oh Lord. And if it wasn't for the inner divinity of awareness consciousness, you wouldn't even be aware of the world of form. It is because of the formless that you're aware of form. So there's no point of worshiping form because it's because of the formless that you can ever begin to experience the divinity of all of existence.

— —

CHAPTER 4

Advancing Your Consciousness in This Technological Age

Technology is a fast and furious force to be reckoned with in today's society. In this chapter, Dr. Hawkins will share his theories on the trappings and victories of this modern-day phenomenon. He will discuss how you can advance your consciousness alongside the latest technological advancements, such as the media, television, movies, chat rooms, blogs, advertising, and the modern-day marketing barrage we are under. And he will tell you how you can still easily spiritually evolve above all the noise. Throughout, you will learn what to embrace as well as, even more importantly, what to avoid.

When it comes to technology, I hire people who know how to do it. I've never had any interest in computers. The things I want to know are not of a linear denomination. As far as the Internet, it's really the intention of what man has done with it. It can be used for good or bad.

Negativity gets major attention in our society. Bloggerism, television, videos . . . nothing backs up traffic more than an accident on the road. Everybody has to slow down and go, "Oh, isn't that awful?" We are attracted to catastrophes. And what happens then is we get an epidemic of the exposure of this negativity. If you can put together sex, seduction, and violence, you're guaranteed a big audience and lots of money.

So backed by the desire for money, the professionals have found that something that calibrates like 70 or 90 will be popular.

Maintaining Positivity in Today's World

We should reclaim integrity, sincerity, and other virtues. Education was one of the main virtues when I grew up, along with sincerity, honesty, integrity, truthfulness. We saw these same virtues among fellow servicemen in World War II. They were a band of brothers, with a commitment to each other.

So that's a higher level of consciousness. Don't forget traditional America calibrated extremely high. Today's society calibrates barely over 200. So the only thing that brings about any restraint in today's world is the law itself. The reason we didn't lie to each other is because we relied on each other. In today's world, it would be fear of a lawsuit.

That being said, there's still a great deal that's very positive in the media. It can be very educational. The media is the mechanism. It's not the origin. The origin is still the minds of men, so it can be positive or negative.

When I grew up, love was very popular. Now hate is very popular. I think the sensationalism is what leads people.

The Downward Shift in Consciousness

The collective consciousness hit a high in the late '80s, and then began to decline. The consciousness level of Western civilization has fallen dramatically in recent years. And that sort of coincided with the visit of the pope recently, who tried to reconstitute integrity and morality, love and forgiveness, traditional values. These values, of course, calibrate quite high. The pope was trying to replace that which has fallen into disrepute with greater integrity.

The pope got a very positive response everywhere he went, so that demonstrated a certain readiness, capacity, and hunger for the reinstitution of things such as valor and truthfulness and forgiveness, sacrifice, personal sacrifice for the welfare of others, et cetera.

Media and technology have played a significant part in the downward trend of consciousness. As we mentioned, there's a natural tendency, a curiosity, to view negative events. Having viewed it, you don't have to wallow in it or live there. You can see what poverty looks like. You don't have to go there to live.

So you ask yourself, *Where do I want to live?* Do you want to live an animal life? The animal just thinks about food, sex, and territory. I would teach my kids about Freud, about the unconscious and the id and the animal instincts there. If you want to live an animal life, that's where you live. Mankind has an animal side to his nature. It is very territorial and dominant, and is prone to war.

The war side of mankind has resulted in humans being at war 93 percent of the time. And when you look at brain physiology, you see one side of the brain is dominated by animal instincts, which calibrated extremely low, below 200.

Video games, for example, calibrate extremely low— 80. You're going to have to make choices in your life— whether you're going to live at the base of the bottom or the top of society.

The Exploitation of Free Speech

I, myself, am not an enthusiast of free speech. I don't think that everything that can be written is fit for publication. There's the capacity with maturity; it's called discernment. With maturity, I know a lot of things that are legal, but discernment, caution, rationality, a sense of responsibility, social responsibility help you realize that pursuing certain avenues would be destructive.

So the consciousness level of mankind goes down as well as up. It went up progressively during the period of enlightenment. The Constitution of the United States calibrates around 700—the highest of any country in the world ever.

Science is used to save lives. And science is also used in newer and better ways to both save lives and kill people. There's nothing good or evil about science itself; science calibrates in the 400s. It's a linear dimension of reality. It's the nonlinear out of which value comes. So what you're really saying is what should the relationship be between the linear and the nonlinear, because the nonlinear is what gives you the sense of values?

Technology and the Spiritual Path

There's also a certain impatience as you get older. You know what's coming and are ready to get on with it. You're interested in what happens when you leave the body—you're excited about the future instead of clinging to the past. Once you realize the physical body is temporary, you're unwilling to sacrifice everything for it anymore.

You know the spirit is permanent and the body is physical. So you say, "What's next?" You find out whether there is such a thing as heaven. The answer is yes, with different realms.

—‒—

CHAPTER 5

Walking the Awakened Path as a Citizen of the World

In this final chapter, Dr. Hawkins will share his insights about the challenges that the world is facing, and how we as citizens of the world can avoid the pitfalls and bring greater consciousness to our own lives and to the world as a whole.

We'll start out with Dr. Hawkins's thoughts on the purpose of human life.

In my view, the purpose of human life is to serve God, to serve humanity, and to serve yourself; to be a channel of God's will for the good of all of mankind, as well as your own evolution. After all, you are part of mankind, so don't leave yourself out.

It isn't you versus mankind; you are part of mankind. So in serving mankind, you serve yourself as well. The purpose of human life then, if that's what it is, is then the fulfillment of one's destiny—and you fulfill that by service to yourself, God, and fellow man. Love now becomes a quality instead of an emotion. You see people think of love: "Oh, babe, you can't see how I love you." Love is a way of defining one's own reality. It's equality. It's because of lovingness that you step over the black beetle because you appreciate the gift of life—because love is valuable. Love of quality, the essence, and the good. And all of this, as we said earlier, affects how you see and experience the world.

The childhood experiences, then, are the beginning of the building of these stacks. And as parents we need to bring all the beauty, music, and spiritual qualities that we can. All of these end up as cultural norms and mores, whether or not people believe in it. They say, "Well, I don't believe in ethics, and morality, and God, and religion, and all that 1950s crap." And all they're reciting now is what has become a cultural norm in the mores of our current day—the mental impact and programming that goes on. All of this is advanced by technology, and the effect of forms of communication. We have access now to vast accumulations of knowledge. And out of all of that from the house of mirrors, we eventually learn how to sort the wheat from the chaff, and get rid of opinion, narcissism, relativism, and instead develop goals and ego ideals that we wish to become. And then you begin to identify with the models of that. Society needs heroes. Society needs models.

So the current political dialogue calibrates at consciousness level 200. In the generation in which I grew up, the political dialogue calibrated about 280 or 290. So it's of a lower nature, just on the edge of 200, neither good nor bad, and at the same time neither one. It's the influence of the media—people are not interested in what you are in reality; they're interested in what kind of an image is projected of you. And so the projected image is what they are hoping will sway the populace. And as I say, it's done by popularity. Popularity, not by capability. So it's like being the most popular surgeon on the staff—it doesn't mean you're the best one. When I get operated on for a brain tumor, I'm not interested in a popularity contest—I'm interested in expertise.

Our society is not looking at expertise—they're looking at popularity. They figure popularity is what gets the votes, so the aim of the political dialogue then is being very conscious of the media, and then trying to play the media, and play people's prejudices and belief systems rather than lead them. Some people think this is a great emergence forward, but it is not, actually—it's just a play on popularity. We have sexism, racism, and now ageism. So you got all these isms battling each other. And as we say, the minute you add ism to the end of a thing, it drops below 200. So the actual impact of the dialogue is actually below 200, although hypothetically it's 200. The actual impact, as we see with the rantings and ravings on the television, trying to suppress things you don't want spoken because it reflects a bad image, and trying to overexaggerate things that might sound favorable, brings the dialogue below 200.

It's sort of the usual manipulation. The desire for political office seems to be ravenous. Once people are bitten by it, it seems they will do or say anything to get into that office. As I say, the minute you get elected, 50 percent of the people hate you because they all voted against you. The office is so popular because of narcissism.

Integrity is upfront, and then you have character and integrity plus capability. So you would want somebody with great experience and great integrity and a good sense of reality, who understands politics, and who's been in it long enough. None of those characteristics have anything to do with race or gender. Gender doesn't make you a better politician; neither does race or color or age or any of those things.

The Importance of Patriotism

Patriotism is to honor and revere one's country, and one's fellow countrymen, and its historic evolution. The Constitution of the United States, the Bill of Rights, the difficulties it went through in its interpretations by the highest courts. You have a respect for the integrity. When I think of a band of brothers, that was the motif. You would cover each other's backs; you'd die for each other because it's aligned with valor. Valor calibrates extremely high. You stood for the principles of valor, integrity, and courage, and the qualities that your country stood for.

Patriotism is a dedication. In the generation I grew up in, as far as sexism goes, women were honored. Women were respected. So when a woman entered the room, you stood up. Women were revered because of their critical role in the propagation of mankind and bringing up of the children.

The Human Dilemma

The human dilemma is one's alignment with truth. If you constantly choose that which is true, you will end up in a completely different dimension than people who constantly choose what is false, because they end up actually in an alternate reality. It is really not the same reality, which helps you with judgmentalism because you realize the way you experience the world is not the way that person is experiencing it.

What seems to you blatant and obvious truth to them is falsehood. What seems logical and sensible doesn't even cross their mind. The Lord said to be forgiving toward all, and to be forgiving depends on how you see the person. Therefore, when you see the person differently, then you realize they live in a different sense of reality, a different world than you do, and you can't judge them by your standards because they can't even comprehend your standards. We consider mercy, and especially being merciful toward the weak and innocent, as a virtue. There's a whole other culture which threatens our own existence, actually, which sees it as exactly the opposite. Your alignment then has a very powerful effect on how you experience the world, what you interpret as truth or valuable. All your value judgments are coming out of your alignment.

And out of that alignment we're seeking God versus materialism. The spiritual versus the material. God versus the worship of money and wealth and worldly power. And I don't know what people want worldly power for—it seems to me like a terrible nuisance—but a lot of people will do anything to get it. The desire for control is so endemic. Power over others, dominance, hegemony, the whole alpha male syndrome.

On top of all this we have a desire for acceptance and approval from others. *Everybody has to agree with us.* That of course is a narcissistic orientation—desire for approval. You reach a point where you really have no interest in whether people approve of you or not; it's just part of your information whether something is being accepted or approved of, but it is of no personal value. Why is that? Because as you evolve spiritually, you need progressively less and less to the final *you don't need anything.* What do you want at a certain level of consciousness? You don't want anything.

Letting go of desire for approval means that you're less controllable. To counteract that, there's a capacity for gratitude and thankfulness. And as I've mentioned before in other books and lectures, if you just thank someone, and tell them what a great job they did, and how much you appreciate it, it goes a long way.

The shortcut then to spirituality is to develop the habit of being gracious toward all of life in all of its expressions all the time. Being gracious toward life means people have different opinions about things, and you don't have to get up in arms over every insult. After a while you find insults are very amusing. Insulting pieces are written about me, and I think they're hysterically funny.

You're always choosing the high road, mercy instead of revenge. But the value of human life is such that you value the other person's life as well as your own. So when you value life itself, then its various expressions are acceptable. You know that civilizations rise and fall. Right now Western civilization is in a free fall. The consciousness level of America is in free fall. And it's okay with you because over history great civilizations have risen and then they've declined, and they've risen and they've declined. So right now we're in a decline and in free fall.

So we say, well, that's the way it's been since the beginning of time. Great Britain in the early days, and the era of Rome and Greece, and all the great civilizations have risen and they've also fallen. So you accept that all such things tend to fluctuate. Capacity for gratitude and thankfulness, and choosing to be merciful instead of revenge. And we do this because we value all of human life in all of its expressions. And we are very aware that we are mortal and limited. The awareness that we're mortal and limited. Mortal. Mortal means that the days, they are numbered for the survival of the physicality, the body itself. From the dust we arise and from dust we return.

Increasing the Consciousness Levels

You see the ebb and flow in the fluctuation, and high tide and low tide. And it doesn't mean the ocean is coming to an end, you see. It has farther to go before it bounces back again.

When you discover truth and integrity, the thing is to honor and preserve it. Alignment, allegiance, the recognition of the value, and then you preserve it because of its intrinsic value. One has to say, what is the purpose of education and what is it we want? I think if the school has an hour of music appreciation and art appreciation and all that, that certainly fortresses it, and it gives it a respectability and importance.

When we talk about raising consciousness, it sounds purposeful—like we're going to do this and then the consciousness is going to rise. No. What you do is you reaffirm the value of that which is integrous. You reaffirm it by constant respect.

How to Combat Programming

The programming that goes on with you is unconscious. If I ask 20 people, do you think you've been indoctrinated with anything today, half are going to tell me no. The truth is all 20 were indoctrinated today. There's no way you're going to watch the news and not be indoctrinated. We're being manipulated all the time by the media, all the time.

Just being aware of that sets up a safeguard against it. You can decide to remain neutral. You can say, "I don't need to take sides one way or the other." You could say something looks inadvisable rather than saying wrong or evil or something. In other words, even what I'm saying today, if what the world wants is to return to a dialectical materialism in the form of a social justice kind of political indoctrination, it's up to society to do so, but you can't expect then the benefits that arose out of society that calibrated at 440 by indoctrinating people with a philosophy that calibrates at 190.

The second countermeasure is an awareness of the Map of Consciousness. As you go up the scale of consciousness, you're moving to that which is positive and constructive. You're moving into truthfulness, enthusiasm, academic truth, scientific truth. When you get up to 500—is the consciousness level of love. And then 540 is unconditional love; 570 to 580 are very high advanced states of consciousness; 600 is an enlightenment. And from there on you have the great mystics and enlightened beings all the way up to Jesus Christ.

And below 200, you have the negative states, and these are really states of narcissism. So the narcissistic core or the ego is what drives the consciousness levels down. Pridefulness, greed, anger, resentment, avarice all calibrate quite low. And then guilt and apathy, and eventually you end up with suicide, actually suicidal, you lose the will to live.

The third countermeasure to programming is intellectual sophistication—reading the greatest minds in history. Shakespeare of course is a great contribution because he brings up human values and human difficulties, and you begin to see that they're innate to the human condition, not just you, your family, your community, or your country. That what he's talking about is the humanness itself. Whether it's the suffering, or the slings and arrows of fortune, take up arms against them, you see.

Plato and Aristotle are the greatest—and Socrates. René Descartes is of course another. He divided the world *into* and *versus* essence. There's two things going on. And one is the world you think you see, and then there's the world of actual reality, which is independent of your personal views of it.

The fourth and final countermeasure to programming is advancing one's own level of consciousness by following and practicing verified, spiritual teachings and principles of discernment.

What you hold in mind tends to manifest. Therefore, if you hold reverence for God and truth as radiance from divinity, if you align yourself with that which is verifiable truth and integrity, moral integrity, and intellectual integrity, then because you're holding that in mind it will tend to manifest within your life. Out of nowhere arise things that increase your certainty about the validity of that which you are pursuing. Verifiable spiritual truth. There is no higher objective or purpose in living than to realize the highest levels of truth and enlightenment.

The various more-advanced spiritual states are so incredibly rewarding that whatever effort it took to reach them was more than repaid. To live in a state of gladness, to live in a state of gratitude, to live in a state in which you feel a compassion and a love for everyone is its own reward. So you hear the saying that virtue is its own reward. That's really what it means—as your consciousness level advances, your degree of happiness increases. In fact, it relates level of consciousness with percentage of happiness. And the two of them are absolutely and directly related. The higher the level of consciousness, the higher the rate of happiness.

The higher the rate of happiness, the less you need from the world or want from the world. And finally you reach a state of relative independence of the world.

At times there may be a self-examination, wondering, *Am I truly going in the right direction? Is a higher level of consciousness something I actually, really want? Or is it just trendy?* Everybody's into being spiritual nowadays. You'll confront whether or not your spiritual consciousness is genuine.

Final Words of Encouragement

If you are reading this book, you are obviously in a good place. You are interested in Self-improvement and increasing your conscious awareness of reality. Having chosen the high way, people seek teaching, understanding, results of research, things they can confirm for themself. They can confirm it using the consciousness technique itself. And of course the real confirmation is to institute these things in your life, just for their own sake, not for the benefit, but just for its own sake. For the love of the joy that you get out of helping others, you become helpful to others. So everything becomes Self-rewarding. And because it's Self-rewarding, you don't really need anything from others. You don't need anything because you've already gotten all the joy out of it just from the experience itself.

—

About the Author

Dr David R. Hawkins (1927–2012) was director of the Institute for Spiritual Research, Inc., and founder of the Path of Devotional Nonduality. He was renowned as a pioneering researcher in the field of consciousness as well as an author, lecturer, clinician, physician and scientist. He served as an advisor to Catholic and Protestant churches and Buddhist monasteries; appeared on major network television and radio programmes; and lectured widely at such places as Westminster Abbey, the Oxford Forum, the University of Notre Dame and Harvard University. His life was devoted to the upliftment of mankind until his death in 2012. **www.veritaspub.com**

NOTES

NOTES

HAY HOUSE
Online Video Courses

Your journey to a better life starts with figuring out which path is best for you. Hay House Online Courses provide guidance in mental and physical health, personal finance, telling your unique story, and so much more!

LEARN HOW TO:

- choose your words and actions wisely so you can tap into life's magic

- clear the energy in yourself and your environments for improved clarity, peace, and joy

- forgive, visualize, and trust in order to create a life of authenticity and abundance

- manifest lifelong health by improving nutrition, reducing stress, improving sleep, and more

- create your own unique angelic communication toolkit to help you to receive clear messages for yourself and others

- use the creative power of the quantum realm to create health and well-being

To find the guide for your journey,
visit www.HayHouseU.com.

HAY HOUSE
online learning

CONNECT WITH

HAY HOUSE

ONLINE

🌐 hayhouse.co.uk   **f** @hayhouse

📷 @hayhouseuk   🐦 @hayhouseuk

▶ @hayhouseuk   ♪ @hayhouseuk

Find out all about our latest books & card decks • Be the first to know about exclusive discounts • Interact with our authors in live broadcasts • Celebrate the cycle of the seasons with us • Watch free videos from your favourite authors • Connect with like-minded souls

'The gateways to wisdom and knowledge are always open.'

Louise Hay